baseball's new wave

Derek Jeter

Substance and Style

BY
MARK STEWART

Claymont Schools
Intermediate L.R.C.

THE MILLBROOK PRESS
BROOKFIELD, CONNECTICUT

M

THE MILLBROOK PRESS

Produced by
BITTERSWEET PUBLISHING
John Sammis, President
and
TEAM STEWART, INC.

Series Design and Electronic Page Makeup by
JAFFE ENTERPRISES
Ron Jaffe

Researched and Edited by Mariah Morgan

All photos courtesy
AP/ Wide World Photos, Inc.
except the following:
John Klein/SportsChrome — Cover
Kalamazoo Central High School — Page 9
The following images are from the collection of Team Stewart:
The Upper Deck Company, © *1993* — Page 14 top
Pinnacle Brands, Inc., © *1996* — Page 25
Yankees Magazine — Page 31, 39
Gentlemans Quarterly Magazine — Page 33

Printed in the United States of America

Published by
The Millbrook Press, Inc.
2 Old New Milford Road
Brookfield, Connecticut   06804

Visit us at our Web site – http://www.millbrookpress.com

Library of Congress Cataloging-in-Publication Data

Stewart, Mark.
  Derek Jeter: substance and style / by Mark Stewart
    p.   cm.   — (Baseball's new wave)
  Includes index.
  Summary: Presents a biography of Derek Jeter, who was teased as a boy in Kalamazoo, Michigan, for
predicting he would be a great shortstop for the·New York Yankees and who grew up to do precisely that.
    ISBN 0-7613-1516-0 (lib. bdg.)
    ISBN 0-7613-1039-8 (pbk.)
  1. Jeter, Derek, 1974–   —Juvenile literature. 2. Baseball players—United States—Biography—Juvenile
literature. [1. Jeter, Derek, 1974–   —Juvenile literature. 2. Baseball players. 3. Racially mixed people—
Biography.] I. Title. II. Series.
GV865.J48S84   1999
796.357′092--dc21
[b]   99-17935
                                                                                                       CIP
Revised and updated July, 2001

pbk: 3 5 7 9 10 8 6 4
lib: 3 5 7 9 10 8 6 4 2

Contents

Pint-Size Pinstriper

"It was never a matter of wondering whether it would happen—I always knew it would."

— DEREK JETER

hen you were five years old, did you know what you wanted to be when you grew up? Derek Jeter did. He told everyone in his hometown of Kalamazoo, Michigan, that he was going to play shortstop for the New York Yankees. Most of Derek's playmates had never heard of the Yankees; most grown-ups patted him on the head and suggested he plan on being something else. "Even my teachers told me to be more realistic," recalls Derek. Fortunately, Charles and Dorothy Jeter were far more encouraging. "My parents always felt if I worked hard enough I could make any dream come true."

Over the years, Derek's friends and classmates just smiled whenever he talked about the Yankees. Sure, he was a great athlete, but the odds against his wearing the

Derek has incredible focus and determination.
He set his sights on shortstop for the New York Yankees
in grade school and never gave up on the dream.

Reliever Goose Gossage, one of the superstars Derek saw at Yankee Stadium while spending summers with his grandparents.

Yankee pinstripes were so fantastic that they never believed it would happen. Derek's dream even made him the butt of jokes. In his junior high school yearbook, there was a prediction that he would be playing shortstop for the Yanks in 10 years. This entry no doubt got a few chuckles back then, but no one's laughing now. Derek not only did it, he made it to Yankee Stadium three years *ahead* of schedule.

Derek first fell in love with the Yankees in the late 1970s. Most kids in Michigan rooted for the Detroit Tigers, but Derek and his younger sister, Sharlee, spent their summers in New Jersey, with their grandparents, Bill and Dot Connors. There they rooted for stars like Reggie Jackson, Graig Nettles, Bucky Dent, Lou Piniella, Ron Guidry, Catfish Hunter, Goose Gossage, and Dave Winfield. "I was always a big Dave Winfield fan," says Derek, who remembers hanging a poster of the slugger on his wall. "He was probably the best all-around athlete they had."

Did You Know?

Derek was so homesick during his first year of pro ball that he ran up phone bills of $300 a month talking to his family.

Derek also listened to his grandmother's tales of the great Yankee teams of the past, and of her favorite player, Joe DiMaggio. Grandma Dot was also Derek's favorite catcher. He would coax her out of bed early in the morning, and the two would proceed to the backyard. Derek's cousins remember waking up to the popping of a catcher's glove, as Derek worked on his fastball. Derek may have his grandmother's heart for baseball, but his physical tools most likely come from his father, who played shortstop for Fisk University. "Dad says he was a better fielder than me," smiles Derek, "but he couldn't hit much."

Derek gets his level-headed, cool-as-a-cucumber personality from both parents. Charles Jeter is an alcohol- and drug-abuse counselor, while Dorothy is an accountant—jobs that demand both an even temperament and superior intelligence. These traits no doubt helped Derek through some confusing times as a child. He is the product of a biracial mar-

Reggie Jackson greets Dave Winfield after a home run. Winfield was Derek's favorite Yankee.

riage (Charles is black, Dorothy is white) and quite proud of it. What some might view as a burden for a young person Derek considered an advantage. "No one knows what I am," he likes to say, "so I can relate to everyone—I had friends of all races—black, white, Spanish, whatever. And I didn't go out and say I've got ten white friends so I have to have ten black friends or ten Spanish friends. I had *good* friends. It wasn't a problem for me at all."

Each September, Derek would return from his summer in New Jersey with a new cap or jacket, and a shoe box full of Yankee bubble-gum cards. And each year, he got bigger, stronger, faster, and better. In Little League, American Legion, and junior high, he could hit, run, throw, and gobble up grounders better than anyone else on the field. Charles and Dorothy encouraged their son in sports, but made sure he understood that his work in the classroom was more important. They explained to Derek that, as he progressed in baseball, he would encounter more and more boys who had his kind of talent and desire. There were no guarantees that he would be good enough to make a living in sports, so his mind had to be as highly developed as his body.

Big Man on Campus

chapter 1

"Even his outs were impressive."
— KALAMAZOO CENTRAL
COACH DON ZOMER

NBA star Chris Webber, Derek's former AAU basketball teammate.

erek enrolled at Kalamazoo Central High School in 1988, and immediately began making a name for himself as a student athlete. In the classroom, he maintained an A-minus average. On the basketball court, he became the varsity's starting shooting guard. As he reached his full height of 6 feet 3 inches (190 cm), he began playing AAU ball with future NBA stars Chris Webber and Jalen Rose. On the baseball diamond, Derek was simply the best shortstop anyone at the school had ever seen. Some even compared him to another big shortstop, Cal Ripken of the Baltimore Orioles.

At the age of 14, Derek was participating in a league with players 17 to 19 and making them look like children. The owner of a bazooka-like arm, he played on the edge of the outfield grass and threw opposing runners out with room to spare. Someone once put a radar gun on Derek's throws from short, and they were in the high 80s.

As a high-school junior, Derek stung the ball at a .557 clip and clubbed seven home runs. As a senior, he was given almost nothing to hit by opposing pitchers, yet still managed to bat .508 with an .831 slugging average and 23 RBIs in 21 games. Derek also went 12-for-12 in stolen bases, despite a painful ankle injury. And he struck out just once all season. Derek was named the 1992 High School Player of the Year by the American Baseball Coaches Association, and was offered a full scholarship to the University of Michigan. Derek, however, had bigger plans. He wanted to go right into professional baseball.

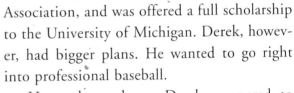

Did You Know?

Derek signed with New York for a $700,000 bonus and a promise—that the Yankees would pay for his college tuition, no matter how long it took him to get a degree. That way, if he were injured and his career cut short, he would still be assured of a top-notch education.

How advanced was Derek compared to other high-school prospects? In truth, no one knew for sure. Pro teams looked at his numbers and wondered if he was as good as advertised. The overall quality of high-school ball in Michigan is not quite as good as in the warm-weather states, where kids can play all year long. Coach Don Zomer would get calls from scouts in March and April asking how Derek's season was going, and he would have to explain to them that they were still shoveling snow off the baseball field!

The concern some teams had was that Derek's .500-plus averages were fashioned

Don Zomer, coach of the Kalamazoo Central High School Maroon Giants.

*Barry Larkin, one of baseball's all-time greats.
Derek would have served as his backup
had he been drafted by the Reds.*

against inferior pitching. Even Derek admits that his stats were a bit inflated, and that the competition he faced was "pretty bad—nothing like the kind of ball they play in California or Florida."

As the 1992 draft began, Derek waited at home for the phone to ring. He had no clue as to which organization would select him. Although he was acknowledged by almost every team as the best high-school athlete available, the '92 crop of prep players was considered weak, so it was hard to judge where he fit into the overall picture. Among the other top prospects his age were future big-leaguers Johnny Damon, Shannon Stewart, Jason Kendall, and Todd Helton, but none had the projected "upside" Derek did. Actually, the team with the first overall selection, Houston, came very close to picking him. Instead, the Astros chose Phil Nevin, the top-rated college hitter. Derek thought the Cincinnati Reds might take him with the fifth selection, but they opted for Chad Mottola, a college outfielder. That was fine with Derek, who did not relish the thought of trying to replace one of his favorite players, Barry Larkin, the top shortstop in the National League.

When the New York Yankees, picking sixth, announced they had taken Derek, he was in shock. Although he had dreamed of playing for the Yanks his entire life, he did not think they would select him. The Yanks almost never used their top draft pick on a high-school player, and Derek had not had any communication with them prior to the draft. "Everybody said Houston or Cincinnati," he remembers. "So when I was drafted by the Yankees, I had no clue at all. It was actually about the only team I *hadn't* talked with! The phone rang and my mom answered and said the Yankees were on the phone. Oh, man, I can't even describe how I felt."

Sometimes Derek cannot believe how lucky he was in 1992.
There is no way he thought he would be drafted by the Yankees.

Diamond in the Rough

"We're dealing with a very valuable commodity...we want to make sure we handle him correctly."

— YANKEE MANAGER BUCK SHOWALTER

he Yankees had several goals in mind for Derek when he started in the minor leagues in 1992. Defensively, he was already very good, with great instincts and a strong, over-the-top throwing style. Like most young infielders, Derek had trouble making the "easy" play. The plan was to work on his concentration and perfect his mechanics. The Yanks also wanted him to experiment with other types of tosses, because in the major leagues a shortstop often has to get rid of the ball right after he fields it, and may not have time to set up for a big throw. From an offensive standpoint, the Yankees began teaching Derek how to power balls to all fields. In high school, he had used an aluminum bat, which had led to some bad habits. He had a gentle "inside-out" swing, which would not generate enough pop with the wood bats that professionals use. The team hoped that he could learn how to pull off-speed pitches for extra-base hits, but still stroke tough inside-out pitches for singles. Derek was already an excellent judge of the strike zone, and was projected to be a .300 hitter once he mastered these skills.

Unfortunately, in his first minor-league season, Derek came up about 100 points short of .300. He struggled with his new batting style, hitting just over .200. His lack of progress also affected his fielding, as he committed 21 errors in 58 games, with most

Yankees manager Buck Showalter and team owner George
Steinbrenner (above, left). They agreed·that Derek would
not be called up to the majors until he was ready.

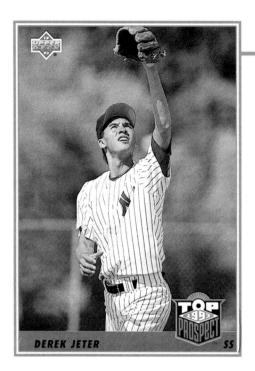

DEREK JETER

Derek got quite a kick out of his first Upper Deck baseball card.

coming on routine plays. "Early on, my problems were all fundamental stuff," Derek recalls. "If you do something over and over, you eventually get better."

Although Derek's stats suggested little in the way of development, the team's scouts liked what they saw. At the end of 1992, Derek played a couple of weeks with Class-A Greensboro, and seemed to work well with hitting coaches Joe Lefebvre and Rick Down. That is where he spent the 1993 season, and under the watchful eye of these two men, he blossomed as a hitter. Derek's average hovered around .300 all year long, and he drove home 71 runs. His base-running improved, too, as he registered 18 steals—up from a mere two the year before.

Derek's 1993 fielding numbers were not as good, however. He committed a whopping 56 errors—the third-highest total in all of pro baseball. Once again, he was messing up too many simple plays. But Derek could also make plays that most major leaguers could not, such as throwing runners out from his knees, and going deep in the hole between short and third to take away sure hits. He knew what it was going to take to round out his game: a lot more practice. Derek understood that steadying his defense

"Any kind of error you can think of, I made!"
DEREK JETER ON HIS 1993 SEASON

meant fielding thousands of grounders and making thousands of throws—a daunting proposition that many young players shy away from. "I think it comes easy to work hard," he says. "I was always taught, don't short-change yourself. Keep working to get better."

Aside from practice, what Derek needed most was a little confidence-booster. He received it from none other than Gene Michael, the general manager of the New York Yankees. Back in the 1960s, Michael had been a shortstop in the Pittsburgh Pirates farm system and committed more than 50 errors a year in his first 3 pro seasons. He paid a visit to Greensboro halfway through the 1993 season, at which point Derek had already committed 35 errors. Michael explained to Derek that he had to relax, yet not so much that he became careless. In other words, he had to find his "comfort zone." This was what had enabled Michael to make the majors, and what had kept him there for 10 seasons. He simply suggested that Derek ease up a bit. You can only get

Derek owes a lot to Gene Michael, who told him to just relax and play ball.

one out per throw, Michael joked, so why send a cannon shot to first when one isn't needed? After that, Derek cut down on his errors by nearly half.

Derek remembered this lesson when he was invited to join the major-league club for the first time, during spring training in 1994. Although the Yankees had Derek ticketed for the minors again, the team wanted him to start "rubbing elbows" with his future teammates. He was now carrying himself like a polished pro, although it was not always easy to find his comfort zone surrounded by so many stars. Derek was still only

This is the type of throw the Yankees taught Derek in the minors.

19 years old, and often in awe of his surroundings. "I'm going from Kalamazoo Central High School, with a friend of mine at third and another friend of mine at first, and here I am in spring training, with Wade Boggs to my right, and I'm throwing to Don Mattingly," he laughs. "I couldn't believe it!"

That season, the hard work and sound advice began paying huge dividends, as Derek finally put it all together and had a spectacular year. Beginning 1994 at Class-A Tampa, he batted .329 in a league that is traditionally tough on hitters, and also swiped 28 bases in just 69 games. The organization promoted Derek to Class-AA Albany at the end of June, and he continued to punish pitchers with a .377 average. The Yankees are usually conservative when it comes to moving a player through their system quickly, but in Derek's case they had no choice but to make an exception. Six weeks after arriving at Albany, he packed his bags for Columbus, Ohio, and joined New York's top farm team, the Clippers. Although he played well at each stop, Derek says moving so rapidly through the farm system was not easy. "There's always a transitional phase you have to go through whenever you move from one level to a higher level," he explains. "I had to make adjustments at each. The pitchers have more control. You've got to be more patient. You really have to try to learn the strike zone and not get yourself out."

Derek was one of the youngest players in the International League, yet he handled himself like an old pro, hitting .349 for Columbus and making all the plays in the field. In any other year, he might have been promoted all the way to the majors. But a bitter labor dispute halted the big-league season in August, and it

Tony Fernandez, the veteran shortstop who was signed by the Yankees while Derek developed in 1995.

never resumed. Derek finished 1994 with a combined batting average of .344, with 43 extra-base hits and 50 steals in 55 attempts. His season was so good that *Baseball America*, *The Sporting News*, *Baseball Weekly*, and Topps all named him the top player in the minors. He was also named MVP of the Florida State League, despite having played just 69 games with the Tampa team. "I was fortunate to do well," Derek says modestly. "My goal wasn't to go out and win the Player of the Year award, my goal was to have a good season. And that's what I did."

Did You Know?

One of Derek's biggest baseball thrills was meeting Rachel Robinson, the wife of Jackie Robinson, who broke Major League Baseball's "color barrier" in 1947. "I wouldn't be where I am today if it weren't for Jackie Robinson," he says. "It's something I'll never forget."

Derek went to spring training in 1995 and turned a lot of heads with his play. The Yankees had started the previous four seasons with four different shortstops, so it was very tempting to promote their shortstop of the future. Instead, the team signed veteran Tony Fernandez so Derek could get a full year at Class-AAA. Derek was told he must show consistency in the field and increase his power at the plate. If he did these things, he would be the team's Opening Day shortstop in 1996.

minor-league *stats*

Season	Level	AB	H	R	2B	3B	HR	RBI	SB	BA
1992	A	210	44	23	10	0	4	29	2	.210
1993	A	515	152	85	14	11	5	71	18	.295
1994	A–AA–AAA	540	186	103	27	11	5	78	50	.344
1995	AAA	486	154	96	27	9	2	45	20	.317

Derek responded with another terrific year. He batted .317 with 27 doubles and 9 triples in 123 games, and led the International League in runs scored with 96. His throwing was still a bit erratic, but by season's end he was playing relaxed and confident defense. During 1995, Derek was called up twice by the Yankees. The first promotion came in May, when Fernandez went on the disabled list with a strained rib-cage muscle. Derek returned to Columbus when Fernandez was healthy. "It was a dream come true," he says of his first stint in the majors. "It's tough to put into words and explain how I felt. The only thing that hurt a little was I was sent down before we went to play in Detroit. A lot of my friends and family were going to come see me."

Derek rejoined the Yanks in September, after the minor-league season was over. The team was making a run for the World Series, and Derek was there primarily to soak up the atmosphere and feel what it is like to be in a pennant race. He claims he actually learned more sitting on the bench than he had earlier in the season, as a regular. "The second time around I saw everything," Derek says, "because I *didn't* play."

Derek poses in the Yankee Stadium dugout with his
1994 Baseball American Minor League Player of the Year award.

Slow Start, Fast Finish

chapter 4

"We may suffer some growing pains going into this thing, but our plan is to make Derek our starter."

— JOE TORRE

hen Derek arrived at spring training in 1996, the Yankees had a new manager, Joe Torre. An All-Star catcher and infielder during the 1960s and 1970s, Torre held a record he was anxious to let someone else have: No one in baseball history had been involved in more games as a player, coach, or manager without reaching the World Series. He knew that one of the keys to snapping this streak was to develop Derek quickly. He told the young shortstop that—as long as he made the routine plays in the field—the starting job was his.

Torre was hoping to give Derek a shot of confidence, but the strategy backfired. Throughout training camp, Derek battled a severe case of nerves. His footwork was terrible, his throws to first base were all over the place, and he seemed to be looking over his shoulder at the slick-fielding Fernandez, who had been relegated to backup duty with Derek's arrival. The job

> ## Did You Know?
>
> Derek's locker is located next to the one that belonged to the late Thurman Munson. Munson was the last first-round pick until Derek to become a star player for the Yanks.

might have been Derek's, but Torre had a great insurance policy just in case he was not ready.

That situation changed a week before the regular season began, when Fernandez broke his elbow diving for a ground ball. Now it was do or die with Derek. Rising to the challenge, he finally began to play up to his abilities. In the season's first game, against the Cleveland Indians, Derek became the first Yankee rookie to hit a homer on Opening Day in 25 years, blasting a Dennis Martinez pitch out of Jacobs Field. He also made a play in the seventh inning that erased any doubt that he had a major-league glove. Cleveland's Omar Vizquel chipped a David Cone pitch into the outfield—too short for leftfielder Gerald Williams to catch and seemingly too far for Derek to track down. Derek, however, had spun around and was in full stride an instant after Vizquel made contact. Pitcher David Cone watched from

Joe Torre, whose calm demeanor helped Derek stay focused during his first full season with the Yankees.

the mound in awe as the rookie raced into shallow left and the ball settled into his outstretched glove. Derek said later that he was not sure how he made the play look so easy; he just remembered making up his mind that he was going to catch the ball. Months later, Cone remarked the Yankees learned something important about their new shortstop that day: He was not afraid to make a big-time play.

Normally, a highly touted rookie for the New York Yankees is the subject of intense scrutiny by the fans and the media. But in the spring of 1996, no one paid much attention to Derek, who was quietly doing his job in the field and handling himself well at the plate. The headlines were instead dominated by the team's lusty hitting and rusty pitching. Paul O'Neill and Wade Boggs were in the hunt for the batting title, Bernie Williams was having a breakout season, and Tino Martinez was driving in runs in bunches. The Yankee hurlers, however, were getting pounded. None of the starters had an ERA under 4.00, and only middle reliever Mariano Rivera was having a good start. Torre knew that his pitchers eventually would come around, so he did not worry too much. And he loved the fact that the press was too preoccupied to put the magnifying glass on Derek. As far as the manager was concerned, the less attention the media paid to his young shortstop, the more time he had to gain confidence and find his comfort zone.

Rey Ordonez of the Mets. He and Derek gave New Yorkers plenty to talk about in 1996.

Something else that helped take the focus off Derek was that the New York Mets had a rookie shortstop named Rey Ordonez, who was batting over .300 and making eye-popping fielding plays. The last time the city had two young shortstops this good was way back in the 1940s, when the Yankees were breaking in Phil Rizzuto and the Brooklyn Dodgers promoted Pee Wee Reese to the big leagues. Rey and Derek were hardly strangers. In fact, they had known full well that they would one day be playing for rival teams. "Rey can pick it," says Derek, "no doubt about it. We came up in the minors together and played against each

"One of the best things about being a Yankee is that you have guys like Whitey Ford, Phil Rizzuto (seen here throwing out the first ball in spring training), Ron Guidry, and Reggie Jackson wandering around the locker room offering you advice."

DEREK JETER

other. I think it's a good thing to have a little competition, it spurs you on. I follow Rey as I do all my friends, such as Alex Rodriguez in Seattle, Alex Gonzales in Toronto, and a lot of other players I have played against." The baseball world finally began to notice Derek after the All-Star break, when he picked up his level of play. Typically, a rookie who gets off to a good start suffers a slump after midseason, as opponents are able to find "holes" in his game. Well, there were no holes in Derek's game. In fact, he kept getting *better*. He hit .350 in the second half, and moved from the bottom of the batting order into the number-two slot. His discipline at the plate kept many an inning alive, and his power stroke really came around. During a crucial 10-week stretch, when the Yankees seized control of the division race, Derek batted over .375. The Baltimore Orioles hung tough until the end, winning 88 games to New York's 92, which was enough to secure the Wild Card spot in the playoffs. Thanks in no small part to Derek, the Yankees had their first division title in 15 years.

Derek finished the season with 25 doubles, 6 triples and 10 homers. His .314 average and 104 runs were both second on the team, and he led the Yankees in hits with 183. When the votes for Rookie of the Year were tabulated, Derek was an easy winner. Derek was also a winner with the fans. He formed a special bond with the Yankee Stadium regulars, signing autographs

Did You Know?

When Derek hit a homer on Opening Day 1996, his dad had to smile. As a freshman at Fisk University, he hit a homer in his first game.

prior to games and even chatting with them while kneeling in the on-deck circle. "Sometimes I ask them if I should bunt, or I might ask them if I should swing at the first pitch," he says. "When the fans talk, I talk back—I don't believe in ignoring anybody."

Derek gets a hug from his dad at the news conference called to announce his unanimous selection as 1996 American League Rookie of the Year.

Pressure Player

"You just couldn't have written a better script if you'd been in Hollywood."

— DEREK JETER

s the Yankees prepared for the playoffs, fans began to analyze New York's chances of making it to the World Series. The pitching staff, everyone agreed, was now in excellent shape, as was the defense. The team had no obvious superstar on offense, yet its lineup was packed with the kind of tough, experienced players who traditionally perform well under postseason pressure. Thus, by process of elimination, the player on the spot would be Derek. Because he had just one season of major-league experience, he was considered New York's only weak link. If he did not produce as he had throughout the year, the team might be in trouble.

In the opening game of the playoffs against the Texas Rangers, it certainly looked as if the doomsayers would be right. Derek left six runners on base, and the Yankees lost. The New York newspapers were screaming for Torre to drop him out of the two-spot before he did any more damage to the team's World Series chances. "Early on in the Texas series, everybody said I was a rookie and I was nervous and I choked on the pressure," Derek remembers.

Derek's 1997 Score baseball card shows a confident young star.

Derek scores the winning run against the Rangers in Game Two of the 1996 Divisional Playoffs.

Torre knew something, however, that the press did not: Derek was mature enough to put a bad day behind him and come back strong. In Game Two against Texas, the Rangers went right at Derek, hoping to humiliate him and eliminate him as a factor in the series. But just as Torre had hoped, it was Derek who made the Rangers look bad, picking up three hits and scoring the winning run in a dramatic extra-inning victory. Derek finished the series with a .412 average, and the Yankees beat Texas in four games.

In the American League Championship Series, Derek continued his hot hitting against the Baltimore Orioles. He batted .417 against Baltimore pitching, including a disputed home run in Game One. With the Yankees trailing 4–3 in the eighth inning, Derek lifted a fly ball into Yankee Stadium's right-field corner. Tony Tarasco sprinted to the wall and jumped to catch it, but a 12-year-old fan leaned over the railing and deflected the ball into the stands. Umpire Richie Garcia had a poor angle on the play, and called Derek's hit a home run. The Yankees went on to win the game in 11 innings, and took the series 4 games to 1, with Derek recording the final out with a diving stop of a Cal Ripken grounder. In his first full season as a major leaguer, Derek had helped his team to the pennant!

When the World Series started, no one was questioning Derek's ability to contribute under pressure anymore. Against one of the great pitching staffs in history, he came to the plate 24 times and reached base 9 times. In Game Four, with the Yanks down 2 games to 1 and trailing 6–0 in the sixth inning, Derek got lucky again. He hit a foul pop-up down the right-field line that looked like a certain out. But umpire Tim Welke got in the way of Atlanta's Jermaine Dye, preventing him from catching the ball. Given new life, Derek laced a single that ignited a three-run rally. The Yanks later tied the game on a dramatic homer by Jim Leyritz, and in the top of the tenth inning, Derek got a clutch hit to put a man into scoring position. He later came around to score, and New York held on for the win.

> ## Did You Know?
>
> *Derek started the **Turn 2 Foundation** for troubled kids in 1996. His father now runs it.*

*You can't win 'em all. Derek fails to snare a hit by
Terry Pendleton in a Game Two loss to the Braves in the 1996 World Series.
The Yankees came back to sweep the next four games and win the championship.*

The Yankees also won Game Five to take a 3–2 lead. In Game Six, Derek knocked in a run against four-time Cy Young Award winner Greg Maddux to help the Yankees win the world championship. During the series, Derek led the team with five runs. He also established a new postseason mark for rookies, with a total of 22 hits. After the final out, Derek raced to the mound and joined the celebration. Then he made his way through the clubhouse and opened the door to find his family waiting. He threw his arms around Dot and gave her a big, champagne-soaked hug.

Derek hugs pitcher John Wetteland after he closes out a tense 3–2 victory in Game Five of the 1996 World Series.

Derek—the
Old Pro

Despite his age, Derek earned the kind of respect normally reserved for veterans. Here's what some Yankees past and present have to say about him:

"He's 'baseball bright.' He knows the game and he respects the game."

WILLIE RANDOLPH,
YANKEES COACH

"The kid is amazing. He plays like a guy who's been around for 10 years."

HALL OF FAMER PHIL RIZZUTO

"Derek knows how to be serious, and he knows how to have fun."

MANAGER JOE TORRE

"I like the way he carries himself....Derek is already a veteran."

DAVID CONE, TEAMMATE

You Can't Win 'Em All

chapter

"I'm trying to think who the best Yankee shortstop I've ever seen is, and I keep coming back to this kid."

— HALL OF FAME SHORTSTOP PHIL RIZZUTO

Derek's second full season in the majors saw him make the kind of progress every team hopes for. Often, a star rookie struggles the following year—opponents have all winter to analyze and dissect his game, while the player himself tends to let up just a bit. In Derek's case, all he did was work harder and get better. He became more aggressive at the plate, banging out 190 hits, yet also learned to be more selective, increasing his walk total from 48 to 74.

Derek also became a much more polished shortstop, learning how to play different hitters in different situations, and getting a better feel for when to take his time and when to hurry. He led the American League with 457 assists and cut his errors from 22 to 18. Practice and experience had much to do with his improvement on defense, but in his mind a lot had to do with attitude. "It's about wanting the ball hit to you," Derek explains, adding that "you have to know what you can do and play 'within yourself.' If you do mess up, you try not to make the same mistake again."

On paper, the 1997 Yankees were every bit as good as the 1996 team. But defending a championship is not easy. Teams threw everything they had against the Yankees, playing every game as if the pennant were on the line. The New York pitching staff was good, but not great, and the offense was not always able to come up with the big hit. At midseason, the team was in second place behind the high-flying Orioles, seven games back. Not much changed the rest of the way, and by the time New York mounted a serious assault on first place, it was too late.

The good news was that the Yankees had the best second-place record of any A.L. team, which meant they qualified for the playoffs as the Wild Card team. The bad news was that they had to play the red-hot Indians. With New York up 2 games to 1 and needing just four more outs to steal the best-of-five series, the Indians tied Game Four with a dramatic homer in the eighth inning, then won it the ninth on a single that glanced off pitcher Ramiro Mendoza's glove. The hit barely eluded Derek, who made a full-out dive to glove the ball; he can still see it rolling when he closes his eyes.

The deciding game also went to the Tribe, 4–3, putting a disappointing end to the Yankees season. Derek played great baseball against Cleveland, with a pair of home runs and an on-base percentage close to .500. The first homer, in Game One, came sandwiched between round-trippers by Tim Raines and Paul O'Neill. It marked the first time a team had gone back-to-back-to-back in the history of postseason play. Unfortunately, personal accomplishments and all-time records do not mean much when you are watching someone else play the World Series on TV. Losing the Cleveland series was one of the worst feelings Derek ever had.

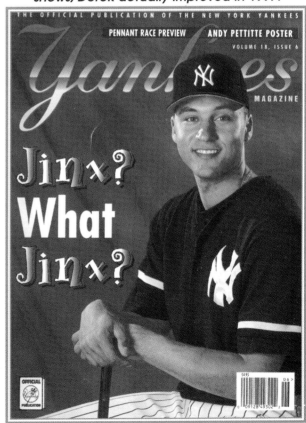

Many players suffer a "Sophomore Jinx" after a great rookie year. As this issue of Yankees Magazine shows, Derek actually improved in 1997.

chapter

Unstoppable

"I can't see anybody dominating the league the way we did."

— DEREK JETER

he Yankees began 1998 on a mission to make up for their failures of 1997. Nothing short of a World Series victory would satisfy the players, so they worked extra-hard in spring training. The result was three straight losses to open the season, and fear among fans that the club's tempestuous owner, George Steinbrenner, might start telling manager Joe Torre how to run the team. Steinbrenner did not want the Orioles to run away with the division again, which was a distinct possibility. Baltimore owner Peter Angelos had

Did You Know?

Derek and Alex Rodriguez are best friends. They first met in 1993, when Rodriguez was a high-school senior and Derek was beginning his second year of pro ball. Although they did not play each other in the minors, they did keep in touch. In 1996, when both burst upon the major-league scene, they stayed in each other's apartments whenever their teams played. Since then, they have vacationed, partied, played hoops, and hung out together on a number of occasions. "We enjoy competing against each other," says Derek. "When he hits a home run, he'll go sit on the bench and flex his arms at me."

assembled quite a group of veteran players over the winter, and could now field a lineup loaded with All-Stars.

The Yankees, however, had responded to these moves with some squad-strengthening transactions of their own. To Derek's left was a new second baseman, Chuck Knoblauch. Like Derek, he was a former Rookie of the Year for a world championship team (the 1991 Twins), and an above-average hitter for a middle infielder. To Derek's right was a new third baseman, Scott Brosius. A former shortstop, Brosius had great range at the "hot corner," meaning Derek could cheat a step toward the middle of the diamond and perhaps take away a few hits up the middle. The Yankee pitching was also much improved. David Wells and Hideki Irabu—both erratic in 1997—showed better consistency and balance in their spring starts. Also, an intriguing newcomer, Orlando "El Duque" Hernandez, was ready to step in if anyone in the starting rotation faltered.

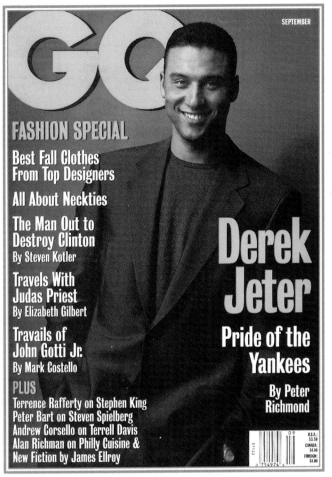

Being one of New York's most handsome and stylish young men has its benefits. In September 1998, Derek made the cover of GQ magazine.

The Yankees survived their bumpy beginning and finished April with a 17–6 record. In May, the team stayed hot and won 20 of 27 games to open up a $7\frac{1}{2}$-game lead on the Red Sox in the Eastern Division. Wells pitched a perfect game against the Twins on May 18th, providing the first highlight in what would soon become a historic season. In June, the Yankees continued to crush their opponents, winning another 19 games. In July, New York all but ended the division race by going 20–7. Derek batted .337 for the month, with 5 doubles and 4 home runs.

Derek relaxes with third baseman Scott Brosius prior to their 1998 playoff game against the Rangers. Thanks to these two, the left side of the New York infield was airtight in 1998.

As August began, Derek was leading the American League in runs scored, and was second in hits and batting average. Tino Martinez and Paul O'Neill were each on a 100-RBI pace, and Bernie Williams was hitting over .350. The pitching staff was untouchable, with three potential 20-game winners, and Mariano Rivera was automatic out of the bullpen. New York's record stood at 76–27, putting them within striking distance of the league mark for wins in a season. In 1954 the Cleveland Indians finished with 111 victories during the regular season. To break that record, the Yankees needed to win 36 of their remaining 59 games.

In August the team won 22 more games, and on September 4, the Yankees won their 100th game. No team had ever reached the "century mark" that quickly. New York scored another 14 victories, giving them 114 for the year.

Derek has a tremendous amount of talent. The sky's the limit for him."
CHUCK KNOBLAUCH

Derek finished the season with a flourish, too, placing among the A.L. leaders in several offensive categories. His final numbers were 127 runs (1st), 203 hits (3rd), eight triples (4th), and a .324 batting average (5th). Derek also reached career highs with 19 homers, 84 RBIs, 30 steals, and a .481 slugging average. He was most proud, however, of his fielding stats. Derek committed just nine errors—evidence of his relentless drive to improve. Despite the fact that his team was winning its division by a record margin, he never stopped tinkering with his game. "I'm not one to sit around and be satisfied about something," Derek says. "I can always get better."

Derek slides into home with his spikes high, knocking the catcher's foot off the plate. Old-time players love his super-competitive style.

Icing on the Cake

"It's not like a team that blows you away—they just play baseball and beat you any way they have to."
— Padres coach Merv Rettenmund

With 114 regular-season wins, the 1998 Yankees were being called one of the greatest teams ever. Many felt they were the most perfectly balanced collection of players in history. That meant nothing, of course, if the team could not win the World Series—they would just be another good club that choked under pressure. Many believed the strain of contending for the imaginary "best-ever" title would prove the team's undoing. But as Derek is quick to point out, he and his teammates were focused on the challenges ahead, not on what they had already accomplished. "A lot of people let other factors pressure them," he explains. "The only pressure you have is what you put on yourself."

*Derek knows when to bear down and when to loosen up.
He and Tim Raines share a laugh before Game Six of the
1998 A.L. Championship Series against the Indians.*

Derek belts a two-run triple against the Indians in the 1998 A.L. Championship Series. This hit put the game out of reach, giving the Yankees their second pennant in three years.

The only pressure the Yanks put on themselves was the necessity of defeating their next opponent, the Texas Rangers. It was a team that matched up well with the Yankees on paper; the league's MVP, Juan Gonzalez, anchored a potent offensive lineup, and the Rangers had three excellent starting pitchers. But the Yankees countered as they had all season long, with David Wells, David Cone, and Andy Pettitte limiting Texas to just one earned run in a three-game sweep.

The Jeter File

DEREK'S FAVORITE...

Music	Rhythm and Blues
Musician	Mariah Carey
Actor	Samuel L. Jackson
Super Model	Tyra Banks
Athlete	Michael Jordan
School Subject	Math
Magazine	GQ
Food	Chicken Parmesan
Color	Yankee Blue

Derek's second cousin, Gary Jeter, was a standout defensive lineman for the New York Giants, and one of the top picks in the 1977 NFL draft.

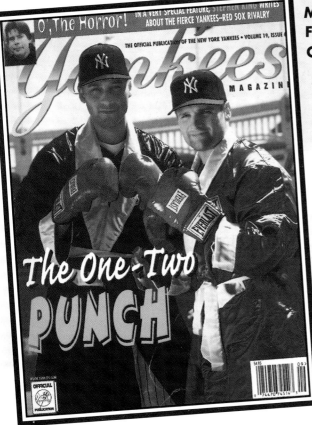

As this YANKEES MAGAZINE cover shows, the addition of Chuck Knoblauch to the top of the New York lineup in 1998 gave the team a terrific one-two punch.

In the American League Championship Series, the Yankees faced the Indians, thirsting for revenge. After splitting the first four games, the Yankees battered Cleveland starters in the final two contests to win the pennant. Derek delivered the knockout blow in Game Six, a two-run triple with the Yanks clinging to a precarious 6–5 lead.

In the World Series, New York faced the San Diego Padres. In Game One, the Padres sprinted out to a 5–2 lead with ace Kevin Brown seemingly in control. But the Yankees got Brown out of the ballgame and stole the opener, with Derek delivering a key hit and scoring the go-ahead run in an amazing seven-run seventh inning. In Game Two, New York clob-

Derek watches Tino Martinez's grand slam leave Yankee Stadium in Game One of the 1998 World Series. Derek came around to score the go-ahead run in a stunning New York victory.

bered San Diego starter Andy Ashby, and cruised to a 9–3 win. The Yankees scored another comeback victory in Game Three, erasing a 3–0 deficit with five runs in the seventh and eighth innings. The team completed a World Series sweep with a 3–0 shutout in Game Four, as Derek scored the game's first two runs. It was the 125th win for the New York Yankees—seven more than any other club in history.

Derek is right in the middle of things as the Yankees celebrate winning the 1998 American League title.

Putting New York's record-setting season into perspective is no easy task. For weeks after their World Series wipeout, sportswriters and fans groped for ways to explain how a team without any major superstars could be so good. Derek believes that the Yankees dominated *because* they had no dominant players. No one acted like the most important guy on the team, and no one was expected to carry the club. The result was a whole that was greater than the sum of its parts. When a game started, no one knew who would get the key hit or make the sparkling defensive play, so everyone just competed as hard as they could. And more often than not, someone like Tino or Bernie or Derek would deliver. With Joe Torre making all the right moves from the bench, the Yankees simply found a way to win . . . 125 times!

Derek is comfortable performing in front of millions, whether he is playing shortstop for the Yankees or visiting The Late Show with David Letterman.

major-league *stats*

Year	AB	H	R	2B	3B	HR	RBI	SB	BA
1995	48	12	5	4	1	0	7	0	.250
1996	582	183	104	25	6	10	78	14	.314
1997	654	190	116	31	7	10	70	23	.291
1998	626	203	127*	25	8	19	84	30	.324
1999	627	219*	134	37	9	24	102	19	.349
2000	593	201	119	31	4	15	73	22	.339
Total	**3,130**	**1,008**	**605**	**153**	**35**	**78**	**414**	**108**	**.322**

* Led American League

career *highlights*

High-School Player of the Year 1992
Minor-League Player of the Year 1994
American League Rookie of the Year 1996
World Champion 1996, 1998, 1999, 2000
American League All-Star 1998, 1999, 2000
All-Star MVP 2000
World Series MVP 2000

"People in here don't have egos...if you come into this clubhouse with a big ego, you'll find out quickly that you're the odd man out."
DEREK JETER ON THE MOOD IN THE YANKEES LOCKER ROOM

Legend of the Fall

chapter

"If he played a year when he didn't go to the playoffs, he'd probably go home and cry!"

— CHILI DAVIS, FORMER TEAMMATE

Once a team knows how to do all the little things it takes to win, it has a tremendous advantage when a championship is on the line. The Yankees proved this in 1999, when their pitching was inconsistent and injuries struck some older players. To compensate, the Yankees' hitters showed more patience at the plate. This resulted in fewer strikeouts, more walks, and clutch hits when the team most needed them. Derek was a perfect example of this. He drew 34 more walks, delivered a league-high 219 hits, knocked in 18 more runs, and scored 134 times. He also hit .349 to come within a few hits of winning the A.L. batting crown.

Did You Know?

Most of the Yankees live in the suburbs, so they can escape the mad rush of New York City life. Derek likes a little madness in his life. He has a beautiful apartment in the heart of Manhattan and takes full advantage of the city's legendary nightlife. He has even hosted his own celebrity parties, like the bash he threw after the 1999 ESPY Awards.

A good stretching routine should keep Derek nimble for many years to come.

The Yankees came together just as the 1999 play-offs began. Against the Texas Rangers, Derek led all hitters with a .455 average as New York swept the Division Series. He also led the team with a .350 average against the Red Sox in the A.L. Championship Series, which the Yanks won in five games. Derek batted .353 against the Atlanta Braves in the World Series, as New York swept them in four straight. This made him the first player since the 1960s to win three championships by the age of 25. Sometimes you wonder whether Derek appreciates how superb his timing has been! "I realize it's difficult to get here," he says of post-season play. "I've just been very fortunate to be on good teams."

Of course, Derek is a major reason *why* his teams are so good. As the Yankees grew older in 2000, many of the team's stars went through slumps and had to play through painful injuries. The one person manager Joe Torre could count on day-in and day-out was Derek, who hit .339 and played great defense despite suffering a couple of nagging injuries himself. He also went 3-for-3 and won the MVP award at the 2000 All-Star Game, getting the start when his friend Alex Rodriguez was hurt. "It means a lot," Derek says of the honor. "At the shortstop position in the American League, you don't know if you're going to get a chance to come to an All-Star Game, let alone star in one!"

After his MVP performance, Derek and the Yankees caught fire and pulled ahead in a three-way battle for first place with the Red Sox and Blue Jays. They hoped to finish the season strong and gain momentum for the playoffs, as they had in past years. Instead, the team finished the schedule with seven losses in a row. Everyone expected them to lose in the playoffs, but the Yankees managed to defeat the Oakland A's and

Derek hits a bases-empty home run against the Mets in Game 5 of the 2000 World Series.

Seattle Mariners despite falling dangerously behind in each series.

That set up the first-ever Yankees-Mets "Subway Series," sending New York's baseball fans into a frenzy. On this stage, Derek performed magnificently. He snuffed out a rally in Game One when he took a relay throw from left field and, spinning and throwing on-the-run, nailed speedy Timo Perez at the plate. It is unlikely that anyone else in baseball could have made this play—or even have thought to *try* it.

The Yankees captured Game One in 12 innings, and also took Game Two, in which Derek collected three hits. After the Mets won Game Three, Torre moved Derek into the leadoff spot. On the first pitch of the evening, he crushed a Bobby Jones fastball over the left-field fence. "I'm an aggressive hitter," Derek says. "I don't really change when I'm batting leadoff." That was bad news for the Mets, who watched Derek slam a triple and score the game-winning run two innings later.

Game Five found the Yankees behind 2–1 in the sixth inning. Derek cracked another home run to tie the score. The Yanks went on to win the game, 4-2, and take their third

World Series title in a row. Derek was named MVP. He said the award belonged to all of the Yankees, and he congratulated the Mets, calling them the best opponent he had ever faced. As for his fourth championship, Derek says it was the best. No one believed in the Yankees at the end of the season, yet here they were atop the baseball world once again.

After just a handful of seasons in Yankee pinstripes, Derek Jeter is already a legend. There may be no better player in baseball when a World Series ring is at stake. What more could Derek do? What more could he want? Nothing, he says, except to continue playing shortstop for the Yankees—a job he considers the best in all of sports.

As for his magnificent work ethic, Derek assures his fans that this is something he will never lose. It is not only part of the Yankee tradition, it has been a part of him since he was a little kid flinging fastballs at his grandmother while other children were still rubbing the sleep from their eyes. "Until I bat 1.000 and play errorless ball," Derek smiles, "there will always be something to work on."

Derek holds up four fingers to signify his four championships after beating the New York Mets 4–2 in the fifth and final game of the 2000 World Series.

Index